YOU REMINDED ME OF EVA LONGORIA!

Youssef Khalim

Copyright © 2015 Youssef Khalim

All rights reserved.

ISBN: 978-0-9787798-4-9
ISBN-13: 978-0978779849

DEDICATION

To: Annie (Inspiration)

Tonya Tracy Khalim and

Runako Soyini Khalim, (my most beloved daughters)

Mother and Grandmother and Great-grandmother, (my most beloved maternal biological ancestors, and spiritual antecedents)

M. A. Garvey (one of my 7 M's: my role models)

Youssef Khalim II; III (my most beloved sons)

Father and Grandfather and Great-grandfather, (my most beloved paternal biological ancestors, and spiritual antecedents).

To: The Forerunners and Reincarnation sources (beloved biological ancestors and spiritual antecedents), and

The Almighty (our Spiritual Father), from whence we come.

CONTENTS

	Acknowledgments	i
1	Not Named	Pg 1
2	The Most Beautiful Creation	Pg 2
3	Fabulous	Pg 3
4	My Friend	Pg 4
5	You're the Best Thing to Have Happened to Me	Pg 5
6	Sparkling	Pg 6
7	When He Made Woman	Pg 7
8	Create Heaven On Earth	Pg 8
9	You Are Sparkling and Gorgeous	Pg 9
10	I Miss You	Pg 10
11	You Are Everything a Man Would Ever Want	Pg 11
12	There's Something Wrong With Him	Pg 12
13	You Have the Most Beautiful Mouth	Pg 13
14	You Are the Dearest Friend	Pg 14
15	Maybe We Could Clone You	Pg 15
16	You Reminded Me of Eva Longoria	Pg 16
17	The Creator Favors Me	Pg 17
18	You Are a Blessing in My Life	Pg 19
19	I Think About You Full Time	Pg 20
20	Best Friend	Pg 21
21	Full Circle	Pg 22

22	How Do You Handle It?	Pg 23
23	Yes, Two Dimples	Pg 24
24	The Body is the Temple of the Living God	Pg 25
25	Your Friendship Makes Me a Better Person	Pg 26
26	Our Friendship is the Most Important Thing	Pg 27
27	You Are the Most Adorable	Pg 28
28	I Love Your Body	Pg 29
29	Your Loyal Fan	Pg 30
30	You Are Very, Very Beautiful	Pg 31
31	I Love You	Pg 32
32	About the Author, and Other Books	Pg 33

ACKNOWLEDGMENTS

To: The Forerunners and Reincarnation sources (beloved biological ancestors and spiritual antecedents), and

The Almighty (our Spiritual Father), from whence we come.

The photos are of Annie, the beautiful and talented *Focus International Hawaii* model.

1 NOT NAMED

You're as beautiful as sunrise,

As pretty as spring's prettiest flower;

Cuter than the cutest girl that you ever saw;

You're feminine, very sexy;

Friendly, adorable; motivational and inspiring.

You're enthusiastic, energetic, and charismatic –

You have a great attitude.

I love the way you walk; and I turn around and watch.

I could talk with you for hours; but the time goes by too fast.

I need a whole portfolio of pictures of you,

So I can keep you in my hands, as well as in my head: Forever.

2 THE MOST BEAUTIFUL CREATION

Women are the most beautiful creation in creation.

And you are living - proof of that.

3 FABULOUS

You have a fabulous personality,

A fabulous smile,

A fabulous walk,

A fabulous body:

And that makes you: altogether fabulous.

4 MY FRIEND

You're spunky, brave; very lovable, and adorable.

You're wonderful, kind, and gracious.

You're so precious and I find:

I'm so lucky - to get to call you my friend.

5 YOU'RE THE BEST THING TO HAVE HAPPENED TO ME

"You're the best thing to have happened to me at this place:"

That's what I thought on the day when I first met you.

Now, I think: you are the best thing that keeps happening to me - period.

6 SPARKLING

They named you aptly, Bertha: which describes you perfectly: SPARKLING!

You're like fireworks on the Fourth of July,

Like shimmering stars in the heavenly skies,

Like the most colorful and beautiful galaxy,

Like champagne, and the fizz in soda-pop,

You are beautiful and lovely; so delightful;

You're pretty, with sparkles,

And when I greet you, say hello,

You light up, from your halo - to *my* toes.

7 WHEN HE MADE WOMAN

Someone will say you look like a million bucks.

But someone else will counter, "No, millions!"

I say you are precious, priceless, sacred, and divine;

Sweet and kind:

Just what our Creator had in mind – when He made woman.

8 CREATE HEAVEN ON EARTH

If we could harness your awesome sparkling personality,

Put it in a bottle, or a can,

Or maybe put you in a pill,

And have people take a sip or a dose of you weekly, or as needed,

We could instantly create Heaven on Earth.

9 YOU ARE SPARKLING AND GORGEOUS

You are sparkling and gorgeous.

I am your admirer, and a fan.

10 I MISS YOU

Yes, I miss you;

I have missed you:

I miss your smile,

Sparkling hello,

I miss your glow;

Your beauty, body;

I miss our too-short conversations,

I miss sensations that erupt when you come near.

Because *your place* was created in my soul,

Without you there, it's just a hole.

Shall I say more? You know the score:

I miss you.

11 YOU ARE EVERYTHING A MAN WOULD EVER WANT

You are everything that a man would ever want in a woman:

Brains,

Beauty,

Character,

An Awesome Personality,

An Angelic Presence – That sprinkles Angel Dust,

A Sexy Body; You Have a Fabulous Walk;

The Most Beautiful Smile,

Inspiration,

Sunshine,

And Sparkles.

12 THERE'S SOMETHING WRONG WITH HIM

If a man who gets to know you doesn't fall in love with you,

You can safely assume there's something wrong with him.

13 YOU HAVE THE MOST BEAUTIFUL MOUTH

You have the most beautiful mouth –

Which men will want to kiss at least a million times.

14 YOU ARE THE DEAREST FRIEND

I was so happy to see you yesterday!

Thereafter, things just went my way.

It's a good thing that I ran out of gum,

So I could come see you, and get me some.

I got a chance to have a brief conversation with you.

And your presence inspired me through and through.

I had the opportunity to see you up close;

And I gleefully got my daily dose.

You are awesomely beautiful, pretty and sweet.

You are the most precious friend - that I want to keep.

15 MAYBE WE COULD CLONE YOU

Maybe we could clone you; then I could get a few copies.

16 YOU REMINDED ME OF EVA LONGORIA!

You reminded me of Eva Longoria.

And you kept reminding me of her, whenever I saw you.

So, I googled her name and looked at dozens of images (pics) of her:

And you remind me of Eva Longoria.

You're both very beautiful, lovely, elegant, pretty, and cute: all of those. *You* have an awesome personality; you're both very charming.

I got to know about Eva Longoria because she was "high-profile" in efforts to re-elect the president, and she was on Piers Morgan's CNN show; maybe even Larry King.

It would be safe to say she helped enormously in securing the Hispanic vote for the president. And she helped raise tons of money.

On Piers Morgan's show she was charming, witty, and very intelligent. (You know she has a Master's Degree). She is also a very successful business woman, and she sells several lines of products through her businesses.

Eva is very smart and articulate. So I had mostly thought of her as "brainy."

When I googled all those images of Eva, I saw that she is also very sexy – and hot! And she knows this.

Like I said, you remind me of Eva Longoria.

17 THE CREATOR FAVORS ME

The Creator favors me.

And He has blessed me through and through.

How do I know this?

I met you.

18 YOU ARE A BLESSING IN MY LIFE

You are a blessing in my life,

Your shining light makes my path bright.

You help me keep my life on track.

So I am back –

To physical and breathing exercises:

And I am rising.

With yoga, you know, I am reviving.

We're ready to make a brand new nation:

Assisting Him in His creation.

You're heaven on earth to those who know you:

Helping us realize what we must do:

Create - heaven on earth!

So the world can have a brand new birth.

19 I THINK ABOUT YOU FULL TIME

I am in school full time,

And I work full time,

And I think about you full time.

20 BEST FRIEND

I will continue to be a best friend – forever.

21 FULL CIRCLE

I have known only one other Bertha in my life.

She and I worked in Robert Washington's three grocery stores, located on the West Side of Chicago, when I was a teenager.

We even went to see a movie together, downtown: " Walk on the Wild Side."

We too, were just friends. She sparkled, just like you. She was a good cashier, clerk, and all around worker, like you. So, life seems to be coming full circle, now that I've met you.

I used to always want my own grocery store – because people will always need to eat.

Speaking of food, you are the nutrition, the sun shine, inspiration, motivation, energy, spirit, and life force that nurtures me - mind, body, and soul.

And I want you – giving me this life, forever.

22 HOW DO YOU HANDLE IT?

How do you handle it when men fall hopelessly in-love with you?

How will you handle it when hundreds and hundreds follow suit?

23 YES, TWO DIMPLES

Thanks so much for the photo.
You are very, very beautiful; lovely and pretty.
You are gorgeous.
I love your exotic and beautiful eyes.
And I love your face.
Yes, two dimples. And I had not seen that.
But I almost always saw you as I approached your cash register,
from the side.
Sometimes, I have been transfixed, watching your gorgeous mouth.
Sometimes, I have been transfixed, watching your fabulous body.
You are well endowed, curvy, and very sexy.
Those sweaters and trousers (your uniform), highlight your gorgeous body.
Perhaps you could let me make it up to you for not noticing your two dimples by letting me kiss each one lovingly, many times, until I can redeem myself.

24 THE BODY IS THE TEMPLE OF THE LIVING GOD

The body is the temple of the Living God,
And again, you are living – proof of that.

Your loving, caring, sharing ways identify you.
So, it is true:

"Our Creator created us millions of years ago, individual souls, with mind, free will and unique personality – a spark of The Light. Male and female, He created us, in the likeness and image of Himself. We are immortal, and we put on bodies – like we put on clothes: to suit our individual mission in a particular life. Our immortality is evidenced in the assertion that after we have been given many chances, many lifetimes to be and do what is right, we are sentenced to hell forever – for persisting on the wrong path."

So, you are sacred, divine, very special and very precious.
Even a certain space around you is sacred ground: not to be encroached upon without your permission.

I love you: spirit, mind, body and soul.
I love the thought of you, the idea of you, your essence, your presence – every scintilla of you, forever.

25 YOUR FRIENDSHIP MAKES ME A BETTER PERSON

You change my body chemistry,
Elevate my soul,

My game:
I'm not ashamed to say how much you motivate,
Inspire me.

You are so sweet and kind,
I have a mind to tell it like it is:

You have charisma: You will be celebrated, discovered:
Become someone renowned:

Maybe become President of the USA, or a corporation:
Nations will love you; the people too.

They'll see that you are smart, intelligent, noble, charming, loving,
caring and sharing.
You're very brave and daring.

You continue to elevate *my* game:
I operate on a higher plane.

And just like I love you, after getting to know you:
Everyone (who is someone) will love you.

For you will make them better persons –
Elevate *their* game,
And make the world a better place.

26 OUR FRIENDSHIP IS THE MOST IMPORTANT THING

While our friendship is the most important thing,
I guess you know I love you.
And since that is not anything new,
It should not change anything between us.

So, friends forever!
And I will never stop being your friend.
Through thick and thin,

I'll be there, caring and sharing;
Telling you the truth: about how special you are:
How you will win the wars, and make it to the top.
I'll never stop - singing your praises:
How I could talk with you for days,
I love the ways you operate.

So, let me state it this way:
I just love the sound of your voice,
And if I had a choice, it would be you.

I love your walk, I love your face;
And I could kiss your mouth for days.

I love your eyes. I love your smile.
I want to be with you awhile.

I love your two adorable dimples.
So, let me keep this story simple:
I love you.

27 YOU ARE THE MOST ADORABLE

You are the most adorable and loveable woman
I have ever met.

28 I LOVE YOUR BODY

You looked really gorgeous today. You are very beautiful, very lovely; very sexy, and you have a fabulous body. I love your body, and I love you.

29 YOUR LOYAL FAN

I continue to be one of your most ardent admirers, your loyal fan, supporter, and a true friend.

30 YOU ARE VERY, VERY BEAUTIFUL

You are very beautiful, exquisitely beautiful, remarkably beautiful, softly and warmly beautiful; deliciously beautiful; loveably beautiful; very sexy, and very, very beautiful.

31 I LOVE YOU

My beautiful, gorgeous, sexy friend,
I love you.

32 ABOUT THE AUTHOR, AND OTHER BOOKS

James L. Robinson, aka Youssef Khalim obtained Unity in yoga on about 7/20/80. He says, "We will recombine into one faith, Judaism, Christianity, and Islam." He has been able to "see" and experience some amazing information about USA presidents Jefferson, Lincoln, and Obama; and also Prophets Moses, Muhammad, and Solomon - in visions, lucid dreams, and in meditation. Khalim makes reincarnation (resurrection) central again in our western religions. He resides in the Chicagoland area. And he is the father of Tonya, Runako, and Noah. His books are widely available and at:
http://amazon.com, http://barnesandnoble.com, http://sunracommunications.com and http://lulu.com

Youssef Khalim's books include *People Of The Future/Day; You Are Too Beautiful; The Resurrection of Noah; You Look So Good; Healing Begins With The Mind; Jubilee Worldwide; Lara, Forever; Tanisha Love; Galina, All About Love; I Call My Sugar, Candie; Natalia, With Love; Svetlana, Angel Of Love; Lori, My Dream Girl; Love of My Life; The Second Coming,* and *You Reminded Me of Eva Longoria*!

www.ingramcontent.com/pod-product-compliance
Lightning Source LLC
Chambersburg PA
CBHW042339150426
43195CB00001B/41